EVERYDAY STEM

ENERGY

Christopher Forest and John Willis

AV2
www.av2books.com

AV2

Step 1
Go to www.av2books.com

Step 2
Enter this unique code

Step 3
Explore your interactive eBook!

AV2 is optimized for use on any device

Your interactive eBook comes with...

Contents
Browse a live contents page to easily navigate through resources

Audio
Listen to sections of the book read aloud

Videos
Watch informative video clips

Weblinks
Gain additional information for research

Try This!
Complete activities and hands-on experiments

Key Words
Study vocabulary, and complete a matching word activity

Quizzes
Test your knowledge

Slideshows
View images and captions

... and much, much more!

View new titles and product videos at www.av2books.com

EVERYDAY STEM

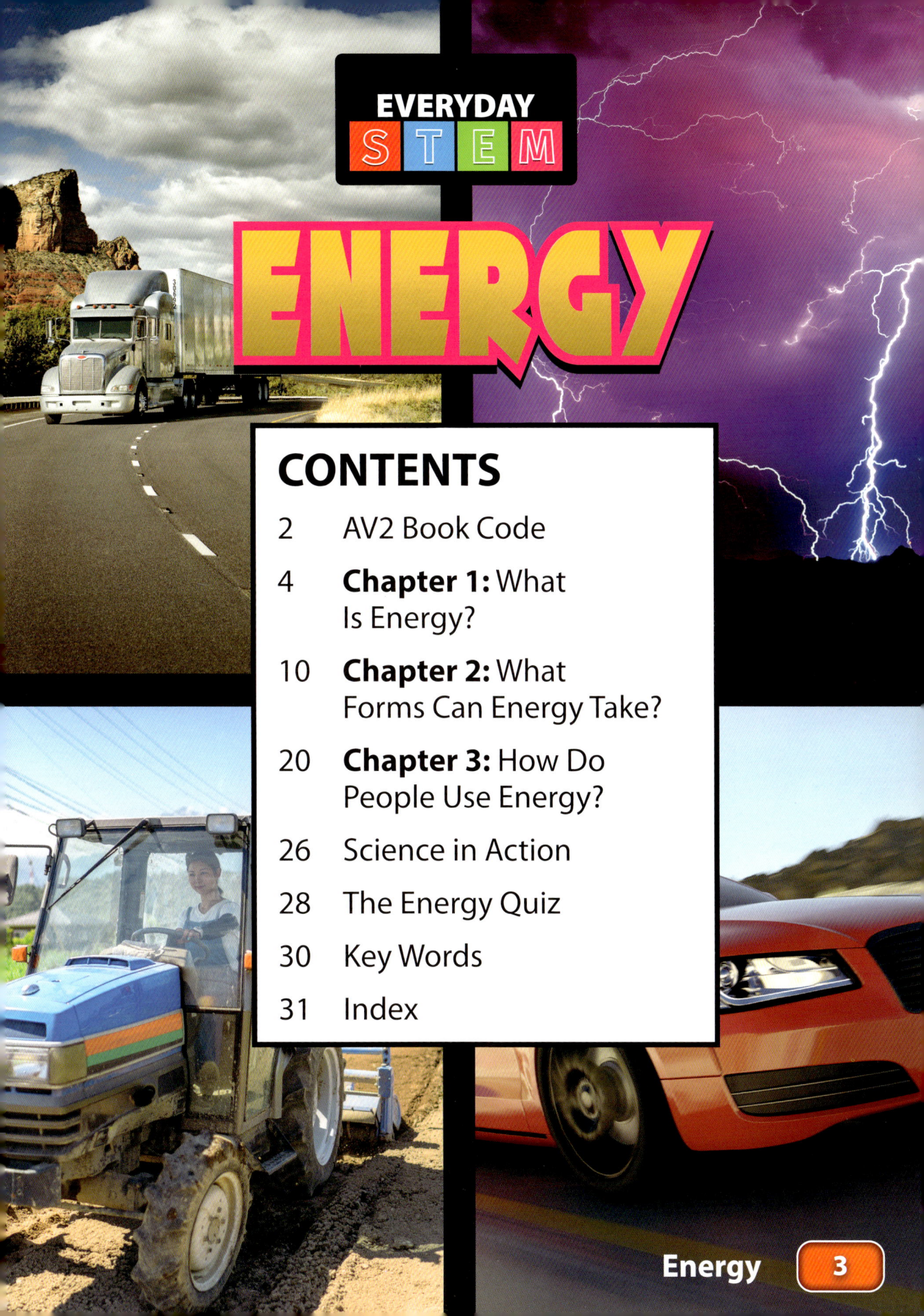

ENERGY

CONTENTS

- 2   AV2 Book Code
- 4   **Chapter 1:** What Is Energy?
- 10   **Chapter 2:** What Forms Can Energy Take?
- 20   **Chapter 3:** How Do People Use Energy?
- 26   Science in Action
- 28   The Energy Quiz
- 30   Key Words
- 31   Index

CHAPTER ONE

What Is Energy?

A farmer wants to plant seeds. First, she needs to make the ground ready. So, she turns the key on her tractor. The engine roars to a start. The farmer drives the tractor to prepare the ground for the seeds.

How is the farmer able to drive the tractor? It is a result of energy. Energy cannot be created or destroyed, but it can change forms.

Everyday STEM

Energy   5

Many things can cause an object's energy to change. One way is if work is done on the object. Work may be done when a force acts on a moving object.

Work can be positive or negative. It depends in part on the direction that the object is moving. Work is positive if the force points in the same direction. Work is negative if the force points in the opposite direction.

Everyday STEM

Plants use energy from the Sun in order to grow.

An engine changes energy from one form to another.

Everyday STEM

Positive work increases the object's energy. Negative work decreases its energy. If the total work done on an object is positive, the object's motion speeds up. If the total work is negative, the object slows down.

We can see work being done in the real world. For example, a tractor uses fuel. The tractor's engine **converts** some of the fuel's energy into useful work. This work allows the farmer to drive.

Energy is all around us. It plays an important role in nearly everything we do.

Energy

Everyday STEM

CHAPTER TWO

What Forms Can Energy Take?

There are different forms of energy. Energy that has to do with motion is called kinetic energy. For example, imagine a boy sledding down a hill. The boy is moving. That means he has kinetic energy.

Think of water flowing in a river. The water is moving. That means it has kinetic energy, too.

DIFFERENT FORMS OF ENERGY

Potential energy is stored in the spring. The red object is at rest, so it has no kinetic energy.

When the spring is released, potential energy is converted to kinetic energy. This shoots the red object into the air.

Everyday STEM

Another form of energy is called potential energy. Suppose you lift a ball off the floor. Lifting the ball gives it potential energy. Think of potential energy as stored energy that is waiting to be released.

What happens when you drop the ball? Gravity does positive work on the ball. The ball speeds up on its way toward the ground. The ball had potential energy when you let go of it. That energy was converted to kinetic energy as the ball fell.

Suppose you stretch out a rubber band. It has potential energy that is waiting to be released. Now, suppose you let go of the rubber band. It snaps back to its original size. This is another example of potential energy being converted to kinetic energy.

Energy

Energy comes from many sources. Humans sometimes use these energy sources to make electricity. People build **solar panels**. These objects use the Sun's energy. People also build **windmills**. These objects use the kinetic energy from wind. People build **water mills**, too. These objects use the kinetic energy from rivers.

Sunlight, wind, and water can be used over and over. These energy sources are renewable.

Solar panels have large surfaces to capture the Sun's energy.

Energy 15

A car's engine burns gasoline to produce kinetic energy.

16 Everyday STEM

Fossil fuels are another source of energy. Humans use fossil fuels often. Fossil fuels include coal, oil, and natural gas. These energy sources cannot be used over and over. When they run out, they will be gone.

Many power plants burn coal to create electricity. This gives people the energy they need to use electric devices. Many cars burn gasoline, which is made from oil. This gives cars the energy they need to move.

Energy

When you touch an object, you can feel how hot or cold it is. This is the temperature of the object. An object's temperature is a measure of how much energy its **particles** have. This is known as thermal energy.

Another form of energy is called electrical energy. Electricity carries electrical energy. This usually happens by the motion of particles called **electrons**.

Energy often changes forms. For example, the Sun gives light energy to plants. Plants use this light energy to grow. Humans then eat the plants. The plants provide energy for humans to do work.

Everyday STEM

Lightning is electrical energy often seen in storms.

Energy

CHAPTER
THREE

How Do People Use Energy?

Energy fuels people's bodies. It helps plants grow. Energy also has many other uses. It is important for everyday living.

For example, people often use electricity to provide power. This allows people to light their homes and cook food. People also burn wood and natural gas. These fuels provide energy to heat homes.

Energy | 21

Trucks use energy to deliver the products we use every day.

Everyday STEM

Energy helps people do their jobs, too. For example, people use trucks to transport items from one place to another. These trucks use gasoline or other fuel for energy.

Companies use electricity every day. This energy allows workers to operate computers and other machines. Builders rely on energy to construct houses and offices. Many of their tools burn fuel or use electricity.

Farmers rely on energy to grow food. Sunlight provides much of the energy that allows plants to grow.

Energy

Riding a bike downhill uses less energy than riding it uphill.

24 Everyday STEM

People also use energy in their spare time. Playing video games depends on electricity. Using a phone depends on electricity, too. A person even uses energy to pedal a bike. The person gets this energy from food.

Energy is an important part of our lives. Everything we see or do involves some form of energy!

Energy

Science in Action

Making Electricity

Is it possible to turn on a light bulb without plugging it in? Do this experiment to find out. Be sure to get help from an adult.

26 Everyday STEM

STEP 1 Go into a very dark room. Ask an adult to hold a light bulb. Make sure the light bulb is unplugged.

STEP 2 Blow up a balloon. Rub it against your hair for about 30 seconds.

STEP 3 Hold the balloon to the light bulb. Watch what happens.

STEP 4 The rubbing makes static electricity. You should notice that the bulb glows. What might happen if you rubbed the balloon against your hair for 60 seconds? What might happen if you used a wool sock instead of a balloon?

Energy 27

THE ENERGY QUIZ

- 1 -
Can energy be created or destroyed?

A. No

- 2 -
How does positive work change an object's energy?

A. It increases it

- 3 -
What type of energy can be used over and over again?

A. Renewable energy

- 4 -
What does an engine do to energy?

A. Changes its form

- 5 -
What form of energy is to do with motion?

A. Kinetic energy

28 **Everyday STEM**

- 6 -
What is energy called when it is stored?

A. Potential energy

- 7 -
Are fossil fuels considered renewable energy?

A. No

- 8 -
Does it take more energy to ride a bike uphill or downhill?

A. Uphill

- 9 -
What does an object's temperature measure?

A. How much energy its particles have

- 10 -
How do trucks get energy to move?

A. They burn gasoline

Energy 29

Key Words

converts: changes

electrons: charged particles that can be in atoms or on their own

fossil fuels: energy sources that come from the remains of plants and animals that died long ago

particles: tiny pieces of matter

solar panels: objects that convert energy from the Sun into electricity

water mills: objects that convert energy from flowing water into another form of energy

windmills: objects that convert energy from wind into another form of energy

Everyday STEM

Index

electrical energy 18, 19

fossil fuels 17, 29
fuel 9, 17, 20, 23, 29

gravity 13

kinetic energy 11, 12, 13, 14, 16, 28

negative work 6, 9

positive work 6, 9, 13, 28
potential energy 12, 13, 29

solar panels 14, 15
speed 9, 13

thermal energy 18

water mills 14
windmills 14
work 6, 9, 13, 18, 28

Get the best of both worlds.

AV2 bridges the gap between print and digital.

The expandable resources toolbar enables quick access to content including **videos**, **audio**, **activities**, **weblinks**, **slideshows**, **quizzes**, and **key words**.

Animated videos make static images come alive.

Resource icons on each page help readers to further **explore key concepts**.

Published by AV2
14 Penn Plaza, 9th Floor New York, NY 10122
Website: www.av2books.com

Copyright ©2021 AV2
All rights reserved. No part of this publication may be reproduced, stored in a retrieval system, or transmitted in any form or by any means, electronic, mechanical, photocopying, recording, or otherwise, without the prior written permission of the publisher.

Library of Congress Control Number: 2020936964

ISBN 978-1-7911-2368-0 (hardcover)
ISBN 978-1-7911-2369-7 (softcover)
ISBN 978-1-7911-2370-3 (multi-user eBook)
ISBN 978-1-7911-2371-0 (single-user eBook)

Printed in Guangzhou, China
1 2 3 4 5 6 7 8 9 0   24 23 22 21 20

052020
101319

Designer: Terry Paulhus Project Coordinator: Priyanka Das

Every reasonable effort has been made to trace ownership and to obtain permission to reprint copyright material. The publisher would be pleased to have any errors or omissions brought to its attention so that they may be corrected in subsequent printings.

The publisher acknowledges Getty Images, iStock, and Shutterstock as its primary image suppliers for this title.

First published by Focus Readers in 2018.

View new titles and product videos at www.av2books.com